Cows Moo, Cars Toot

June Crebbin was a primary school teacher in
Leicestershire, Yorkshire and the USA before
taking early retirement in 1990 in order to
concentrate full time on her writing. She is the
author of a number of books for children including
story books, volumes of poetry and two picture
books, *Fly-by-Night* and *The Train Ride*. June also
writes poetry for adults. She is a frequent visitor
to primary schools, where she gives readings, talks
and workshops. June enjoys walking, reading,
riding on horses or steam trains and discovering
castles. She lives in Birstall, Leicestershire, with
her husband and her rabbit.

Some other books by June Crebbin

Poetry

THE DINOSAUR'S DINNER

Fiction

FINDERS KEEPERS
RIDE TO THE RESCUE

JUNE CREBBIN

Cows Moo, Cars Toot

Illustrated by Anthony Lewis

PUFFIN BOOKS

For Kim and Arielle

PUFFIN BOOKS

Published by the Penguin Group
Penguin Books Ltd, 27 Wrights Lane, London W8 5TZ, England
Penguin Books USA Inc., 375 Hudson Street, New York, New York 10014, USA
Penguin Books Australia Ltd, Ringwood, Victoria, Australia
Penguin Books Canada Ltd, 10 Alcorn Avenue, Toronto, Ontario, Canada M4V 3B2
Penguin Books (NZ) Ltd, 182–190 Wairau Road, Auckland 10, New Zealand

Penguin Books Ltd, Registered Offices: Harmondsworth, Middlesex, England

First published by Viking 1995
Published in Puffin Books 1996
10 9 8 7 6 5 4 3 2 1

Text copyright © June Crebbin, 1995
Illustrations copyright © Anthony Lewis, 1995
All rights reserved

The moral right of the author has been asserted

Filmset in Times

Made and printed in England by Clays Ltd, St Ives plc

Contents

I Saw a Duckling   1

Suddenly Spring   2

Ready, Steady – Moo!   3

River   5

The Stream-dipping Party   6

Steam Train   8

Top of the Mountain   10

My Kite   11

Milk-baa   13

In This Tree   14

Charlie   16

Dandelion   17

The Cow Who Liked Jumping   18

House-hunting   20

Inside the Morning   22

Making the Countryside   23

Counting Sheep   24

Cave   26

No School Today   27

Well, I *Never*! 28

Grandma's Third Leg 30

Conker Collectors 32

Winter Trees 33

Two Owls 34

Frogs 36

Goodnight 39

Cows Moo, Cars Toot 41

A Sticky Business 45

Market-day 46

Wanted 48

Lift-off 50

City River 53

Class 2 at the Dinosaur Exhibition 54

The Peacock Pavement 56

Neighbourhood Watch 57

Hanratty 59

Birdman 61

The Horse Bus Comes to Town 62

Working Windmill 64

Cathedral 66

Wagtail at the Window   68

Playground   69

Boating   70

Leaves Dancing   72

Letter Home   73

Diwali   76

Underground   77

A City Dog's Dream   78

The Seagull's Song   79

Night Hunter   80

Badger   81

Robosaurus – King of the Scrap-yard   83

Cows Moo, Cars Toot   85

I Saw a Duckling

I saw a duckling puffing by
I saw a steam train in the sky
I saw a rainbow eating grass
I saw a cow as smooth as glass
I saw a pond turning round
I saw a windmill leap and bound
I saw a cricket plough a furrow
I saw a tractor dig a burrow
I saw a rabbit in a coat and hat
I saw a farmer with his cat
I saw all these when I went for a ride
Out and about in the countryside.

Suddenly Spring

Today,

bullocks lurched through mud
to feed in the water-meadows,

lambs tottered or skipped
in fields near farms,

flood levels dropped,
streams showed off in the sun,

teashops took down their shutters

and spring was declared officially open.

Ready, Steady – Moo!

It's peaceful here by the river,
All by ourselves in the sun,
Having a chew and a chat now and then,
Moving gently along.

But I'm not too keen on the hikers
That pass through our field each day,
One of them always waves a stick
In a menacing kind of way.

I'm not too keen on their children
Dashing all over the place,
Or their dogs, which run and nip at my heels
And yap in front of my face.

If only they'd just keep going,
If only they'd leave us alone,
Don't they know they're walking through
The middle of our home?

It's time we taught them a lesson,
Yes, but what can we do?
We could try giving voice to the way that we
feel:

Ready, steady – MOO-OO-OO!

It's peaceful here by the river
Now that the hikers have gone,
All by ourselves in the meadow again,
Flicking our tails in the sun.

River

boat-carrier

bank-lapper

home-provider

tree-reflector

leaf-catcher

field-wanderer

stone-smoother

fast-mover

gentle-stroller

sun-sparkler

sea-seeker

The Stream-dipping Party

I went to a stream-dipping party,
With my wellies, a net and a jar,
We waded into the water,
We were told not to go in too far.

Johnny and Ben caught some tiddlers,
And Amy fished out a ball,
Even Dan caught a leaf and a button,
But I caught nothing at all.

So I waded just a bit further,
I could see a shiny bright tin,
I was stretching my net out to grab it,
When I tripped on a stone – and fell in.

I went to a stream-dipping party,
With my wellies, a jar and a net,
Everyone there got something,
But only I got – wet!

Steam Train

Smoke pours from the engine as the steam

Train prepares to leave, clouding itself and

Everyone watching before settling into its journey

Along the valley, close to the river,

Mountains rising in the distance.

Tickety-tack, tickety-tack, picking up speed, it

Races past sheep and cows, bridges, trees,

Aiming for the sea, straight as a rocket, or looping

Into bends, hugging the curve, slowing for the viaduct –

Now, along the straight, smoke flows like a banner.

Top of the Mountain

Up
up
the cable-car glides
and I am inside,
locked in a bubble,
swinging through silence
up
to the top
of the mountain.

Now
we are so high
even an aeroplane

flies below us.

My Kite

On windy days
my dad says:
"Let's fly your kite."

And I say:
"All right."

So we go up the hill
behind our house
and Dad unravels the string
S L O W L Y
while I walk backwards
S L O W L Y
holding the kite.

Then Dad says: "Right,
let go."

So I do,
and usually the kite
goes straight up in the air.

Now I'm not saying Dad isn't good.
He can make the kite do anything,
twist and turn, dip and dive,
a hundred different ways.

"Isn't this fun?" Dad says.
"Just look at it go."

I know.

It's just that I wish,
sometimes,
he'd let me have a go.

Milk-baa

It's not that I wish to complain,
But I can't understand all the same,
Why for breakfast and tea,
Three days out of three,
It's milk – always milk – yet again!

In This Tree

In this tree
are greenflies, sawflies
and beetles burrowing,

In this tree
are ferns and mosses
and a thread of honeysuckle,

In this tree
are butterflies
feeding on sunlit leaves,

woodpeckers
searching for insects,

squirrels nesting,

In this tree
are acorns
and a notice saying:
BULL IN FIELD.

What's that noise?
What's that thundering noise
behind me?

Help!

In this tree
are all these things

and me.

Charlie

In the meadow near our school
A giant carthorse stands,
We feed him crusts and apple cores
From flattened, outstretched hands.

I used to snatch my hand away
From Charlie's lowered head,
I worried that he'd miss my gift
And eat my hand instead.

But now I know his gentleness,
The way he clears my hand,
His muzzle soft as summer grass
Blowing in the wind.

Dandelion

The dandelion clock
Is ready to show
At a puff or a blow
One o'clock, two o'clock,
Three o'clock, four,
Or, left to itself,
This humblest of flowers
Ticks away in the breeze
For hours.

The Cow Who Liked Jumping

There once was a cow
With great good sense,
Jumped over a gate
And over a fence,

Over a river,
Over a tree,
Over a mountain,
Over a sea,

Over a jungle,
Over a plain,
Over a forest
And back again,

Back to her field
And the same old ways,
Chewing the grass
In a bit of a daze.

So was she content
With the usual scene?
Did she go back
To her normal routine?

NO!

She went for the Big One,
Yes, one afternoon
Daisy the Cow
Jumped over the moon!

19

House-hunting

Cottage, castle, bungalow, pigsty –
Which one shall it be?
A cottage with a garden and a paddock for a
                                          pony
Would be just about the perfect place for
                                          me.

Though a castle with a drawbridge and a
                        tower and a cannon
Could be just the thing for fighting off my
                                          foes,
But castles tend to crumble and to tumble
                              into rubble,
So I'd better steer clear of one of those.

Now a bungalow is pleasant, just the right
                                   amount of floor-space,
With ornaments in every nook and cranny,
And curtains at the window made of net so
                                   no one sees you
Going to bed in striped pyjamas like your
                                   granny.

And a pigsty, well a pigsty would be
                                   different and exciting,
And I'm very fond of piglets, truth to tell,
But I think I'll take the cottage with a
                                   paddock for a pony –
And maybe I'll keep piglets there as well!

Inside the Morning

Inside the morning is a bird,
Inside the bird is a song,
Inside the song is a longing,

And the longing is to fill the morning.

Making the Countryside

Take a roll of green,
Spread it under a blue or blue-grey sky,
Hollow out a valley, mould hills.

Let a river run through the valley,
Let fish swim in it, let dippers
Slide along its surface.

Sprinkle cows in the water-meadows,
Cover steep banks with trees,
Let foxes sleep beneath and owls above.

Now, let the seasons turn,
Let everything follow its course.
Let it be.

Counting Sheep

A shepherd was counting his sheep one day,
And this is the rhyme I heard him say:

> One – erum
>
> Two – erum,

That makes four,

> Cock – erum
>
> Shu – erum,

That's four more,

> Skith – erum
>
> Skath – erum,

Into the pen,

> Wine – berry
>
> Wag – tail
>
> Tara – diddle
>
> Den.

Now can you tell me the right amount?
How many sheep did the shepherd count?

This poem is based on a Dorset counting rhyme.

Answer: 20

25

Cave

I have found a secret cave
By the sea, by the sea,
And I think there's no one here
Only me, only me.

From the darkness where I sit
I can spy, I can spy,
The ever-changing light
Of the sky, of the sky.

And I listen to the sighing
Of the sea, of the sea,
And the ghosts of other travellers
Calling me, calling me . . .

No School Today

No school today,
Closed by snow,
We heard it on the radio.

"'s no good,"
We said to each other,
"We'll just have to go
Sledging and sliding
Bravely hiding
Our keen disappointment . . ."

"Yabba-dabba-doo!"

Well, I *Never!*

The other day I swallowed a pig,
It was ever so big,
The other day I swallowed a goat,
It slid down my throat,
The other day I swallowed a farm,
I came to no harm,
The other day I swallowed a bull,
I was really full,
The other day I swallowed a horse,
Delicious, of course,
And only last week I swallowed a hen,
I'm not sure when,
The other day I swallowed my pride
And was sorry I lied
About the pig and the goat,
    the farm and the bull,
    the horse and the hen,
So I started again . . .

The other day I swallowed a tooth –
Now, that's the truth!

Grandma's Third Leg

My grandma has three legs,
And two are flesh and blood,
The other one she leans upon
And that is made of wood.

Last spring, when we were walking
In fields not far away,
She said her extra leg would be
A help to me one day.

And now we're picking blackberries
I know the reason why,
She waves her leg above her head
And hooks the ones on high!

Conker Collectors

Every autumn
my brother and I
shuffle through leaves
looking for conkers.

He bakes his in the oven,
soaks them in vinegar,
threads them on a string
and bashes them.

But I pile mine up
on the windowsill
and just look.

Winter Trees

After rain,
winter trees,
like witches' brooms,
sweep the sky
clean again.

Two Owls

I'm keeping my eye on a baby owl,
Who's keeping his eye on me,
I found him deep in the woods today,
At the foot of a very tall tree.

"He must have fallen a long way down,
But if you look up you'll see
Why he's quite all right where he is," said
                                    Dad,
"And I think we should leave him be."

So I looked up high and I saw two eyes
At the top of that very tall tree,
The baby owl's mum was staring down –
Keeping an eye on me!

Frogs

Down by the river, suddenly
there were frogs
ahead of us, beside us
and, because we stepped very carefully,
thank goodness not under us.

But they could have been;
they were so small
and so like the stones
and leaves beside them;
mustard-green and marbled
with brown.

We watched.
Some leaped in easy stages
back to the water,
others just sat in the middle
of the path,
the only movement
their bodies pulsing.

You would think all of them
would have leaped away
at the first sign
of clomping boots,

but even when we returned
an hour later,
they were still there,
stationed across the path
like markers.

Goodnight

"Goodnight," said the frog, "I am
                    burrowing deep
Into the mud for my winter sleep."

"Goodnight," said the hedgehog, "I'm off to
                    my nest,
It's time I went for a good long rest."

"Goodnight," said the bat, "my feet are
                    strong,
I'll hang in a cave the winter long."

"Goodnight," said the dormouse, "I shall be
Curled in my nest at the foot of the tree."

"Goodnight," said the toad, "I've found a
deep hole
To keep me warm from the winter's cold."

"When you wake in the spring," said the
kindly sun,
"I'll be here with my warmth for everyone."

Cows Moo, Cars Toot

In the fields,
  cows moo,
  grass whispers,
  sheep bleat.

By the river,
  ducks quack,
  reeds rustle,
  fish splash.

In the wood,
  owls screech,
  trees swish,
  hedgehogs snuffle.

Sounds amazing,
  but what is it like
  in the town?

A Sticky Business

On Saturday morning,
Going to town,
Traffic is spread
Thick on the ground.

All different colours,
Red, green and blue,
Stuck to each other,
What a to-do!

Bumper to bumper,
Causing delay,
A streetful of jam
Spoiling the day.

Have to be patient,
Can't turn around,
Slowly we trickle
Into the town.

Market-day

On Saturdays I'm up at four
To go with Bill, who lives next door,
To market,
And while I'm doing what I can
Unloading crates, he takes the van
To park it.

There's heaps of grapefruits big as suns,
And oranges and purple plums
And berries,
Raspberries, strawberries, damsons – lots
Of peaches, pears, ripe apricots
And cherries.

I love arranging nectarines
And polishing their shiny skins
For selling,
But best of all I like the sound
When market traders all around
Start yelling.

Then we're busy all day long
And Bill says I'm his Number One
Best Mate,
And even when we pack away
I'm thinking of next market-day –
Can't wait!

WANTED

TOM PIPERSON
  – for stealing a pig,
NOT VERY BIG
  – that's Tom, not the pig,
BROWN HAIR, GREEN EYES
  – Tom again,
    the pig is pink,
HAD YELLOW BOOTS AND A JUMPER ON
  – that's definitely Tom,
ANYONE SEEING TOM
  – it's a blue jumper,

PLEASE INFORM
THE POLICE STATION
  – or A. Butcher,
    54 Meat Street,
NOW
  – or sooner if possible,
£3.00 REWARD
  – all I can afford,
DON'T DELAY
FIND TOM TODAY.

Lift-off

Going up,
Going up,
Doors closing,
Doors closing.

Level 2.
Cookshop. Curtains.
Bathrooms and Ladieswear.

Going down,
Going down,
Doors closing,
Doors closing.

Level 1.
Menswear. Childrenswear.
China, Glass and Giftware.

Going up,
Going up,
Doors closing,
Doors closing.

Going down,
Going down,
Doors closing,
Doors –

Wait a minute –
I'm fed up going
Up and down
Down and up.

Boring.
Boring.

Right.
Hang on to your hats!

Going up
Through the roof –

Treetops. Chimney-pots.
Aerials and Birdsong.

Going up,
Going up.

Starlight. Satellites.
Moonbeams and Meteors.

Going up,
Going up . . .

City River

wall-slapper

    factory-passer

        rubbish-receiver

            backstreet-winder

                bridge-nudger

            steps-licker

        park-wanderer

    summer-shiner

        ducks-supporter

            choppy-water

                crowd-delighter

                    onward-traveller

Class 2 at the Dinosaur Exhibition

Ann admired the brontosaurus,
Ben began his lunch,
Carol couldn't find her pencil,
Daniel drew a stegosaurus,
Eve examined the wall display,
Frances found a fossil footprint,
Guy got lost and began to cry,
Helen hurried to help him,
Ian imagined meeting a mammoth,
John joined in,
Katie kept on asking questions,
Lee left his bag on the bus,
Mitesh missed the mammoth's tusk,
Nigel noticed it at once,
Oliver ought never to have touched it,
Peter put it back,
Queenie queued in the shop for ages,
Richard reached the end of his worksheet,
Stephanie stood in the dinosaur's footprint,

Thomas took her picture,
Ursula used up all her paper,
Vikram vanished,
William wandered off to find him,
Xanthe explored the way to the exit,
Yasmin yawned and then
Zoë zipped up her anorak and said:

"When are we coming again?"

The Peacock Pavement

Down
These steps,
Beneath the
Floor of this old
Shop, lies another
Floor, a Roman pavement,
Fashioned out of tiny stones
Set in swirls and coils and petals,
And at its centre, a peacock, proud,
Spreading his tail of blue glass feathers.

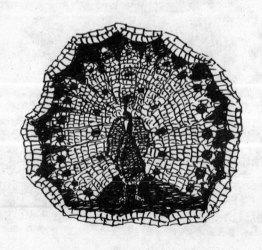

Neighbourhood Watch

If you should wander down our street
Past number thirty-eight,
The chances are you'd see our Flo
Leaning on her gate.

She likes to watch the world go by,
And if the weather's poor,
You'll find her at her window-seat
Or standing at the door.

She drinks in information
Like dolphins drink in air,
"No secret's safe when Flo's about,"
I've heard my dad declare.

"She always knows who's moving out
And who is moving in,
She must have laser beams for eyes,
She doesn't miss a thing.

If aliens came at dead of night
She'd know the reason why,
She's a vigilant observer,
An undercover spy."

"But," Mum says, "when we're away,
It's comforting to know
Our Guardian Angel's keeping watch:
Nothing gets past Flo."

Hanratty

For a long time
The house next door stood empty,
Gates hung off, slates blew down,
Hanratty saw it, liked it, bought it.

My mum didn't like it.

Out of Hanratty's van
From his second-hand shop
Came second-hand furniture,
And five fat ducks.

My mum didn't like it at all.

She pretended Hanratty's didn't exist,
With dustbins in the rose-beds
And ducks all over the place.
She never sits in the garden now.

But Hanratty of an evening
Wanders down his own backyard,
Watches his five fat ducks
Splashing in their paddling-pool –

And I love it.

Birdman

There was a young man of Dundee,
Who lived at the top of a tree,
When asked to come down
By the mayor of the town,
He FLEW down and perched on his knee.

The Horse Bus Comes to Town

I like to ride on the horse bus
That clatters down the street,
I like the sound of the horses'
Clippety-cloppety feet.

"Gentle giants" – Great-Grandad says,
And he remembers when
Everything was horse-drawn,
No motor buses then.

You can sit inside if you want to,
But it's much more fun on top
Watching the crowds of people
Who've come in town to shop.

I can see into upstairs windows,
And across to the Town Hall Square,
Where Christmas lights are shining
In cold and frosty air.

Down the cobbled High Street,
Through the Market Place,
The horses walk in rhythm
At an even, steady pace.

I'd like to ride on a bus like this
Every single day,
I think it's come for Christmas,
But I hope it's here to stay.

Working Windmill

There was a mill stood in a field,
Its head in the sky,
Its feet on the ground,
Its white arms turning round,

And though that field is now a street
The mill still stands,
Its head in the sky,
Its feet on the ground,
Its white arms turning round,

And we can see
Where the grain is stored,
How the wheat is ground,
How the sacks are hoisted up and down,
In the mill in the busy town.

Cathedral

Come into this quiet place where

Angels carved in stone look down on

Tombs of noble lords and ladies.

Here are stained-glass windows to delight the

Eye and tell us tales of long ago – here the Great West

Door and there an eagle spreads its wings. Here are

Rows and rows of seats and high above each aisle

Arches soar. Come into this quiet place.

Listen to its peace.

Wagtail at the Window

There's a wagtail at the window
Tapping on the glass,
Is he trying to tell us
He wants to join our class?

Is he trying to say
That the cold and snow out there
Makes him want to be
Dry and warm in here?

Wagtail at the window,
What you cannot know
Is *we* would rather be
Outside in the snow!

Playground

Our playground is like a cage,
all tarmac and wire netting,
with one small tired tree.

Sometimes we cling to the fence
like monkeys, going jabber, jabber, jabber.
Sometimes we sit beneath the tree.

When we go to the park
there are lots of trees
and we race across the grass like cheetahs.

Boating

Sam and I are hunters,
Paddling our canoe,
In. . .out,
One. . .two.

Across the shining water,
Down a narrow inlet,
In. . .out,
One. . .two.

Past a gloomy forest,
Where the wolves are howling,
In. . .out,
One. . .two.

Round a rocky island,
Past the tumbling water,
In. . .out,
One. . .two.

By the sandy shoreline,
Where the pine-trees whisper,

"COME IN, NUMBER TWENTY-TWO!"

Sam and I, the hunters,
Now that day is done,
Paddle slowly homewards
Towards the setting sun,

In. . .out,
One. . .two.

Leaves Dancing

Once, my mum and I,
going home
through the empty park,
saw leaves dancing,

drifting
in the almost dark,
over swings and slides,

to settle
under street lamps,
like upside-down butterflies.

Letter Home

London, 1347

Dear Mum,
So many years have now gone by
Since first I left my home to try

My luck in London. All is well.
And here's the tale I have to tell:

Found a job as kitchen boy,
Bought a cat for company,

Once, when I was really down,
Ran away from London town,

But as I climbed up Highgate Hill,
The air was there so calm and still,

I clearly heard the church bells ring,
"Turn again," they seemed to sing,

"Turn again, Dick Whittington,
Thrice Lord Mayor of London."

And then I'm very glad to say
Fame and fortune came my way,

Met and wed a girl called Alice
(The house we live in's like a palace),

So, even if, as I was told,
The streets are not all paved with gold,

I'm now Lord Mayor of London, and
Know that you will understand

How much I've missed you. Come and stay.
Come and have a holiday.

From Dick,

    With lots of love to you.

PS The cat and Alice send theirs too.

Diwali

The dark streets shine,
A dazzling festival of light,
The dark streets shine,
Like necklaces of rich design,
Strings of colours, jewel bright,
A song of stars for our delight,
The dark streets shine.

Underground

Nobody told me
that underneath the streets of London
trains rush like hungry monsters,
gobbling up passengers
in their steely jaws.

But they do –
and sometimes they're so full
they have to spit some out.
Which is just as well,
Or I wouldn't be sitting here
telling you –

that underneath the streets of London . . .

A City Dog's Dream

I'd like to go for good long walks
With grass beneath my feet,
So different from the pavement slabs
In every city street.

I'd like to race along a beach
And hear the sea's loud roar,
I'd like to bark at all those waves
Rippling on the shore.

I'd like to rummage round in woods,
Or swim across a river,
I'd like to chase the butterflies –
And maybe stay for ever.

The Seagull's Song

Oh, I do like to be beside the seaside,
I do like to be beside the sea,
I do like to soar above a seaside town,
See the boats in the harbour bobbing up and
down.

Oh, I do like to be beside the seaside,
There is nowhere that I would rather be,
I can perch on sailing-ships,
Grab a meal of fish and chips,
Beside the seaside, beside the sea.

Night Hunter

Starlings gather on rooftops,
chattering like children,

Office-workers hurry home,
heads down, silent,

Lights dim, shops close,
shutters clang into place,

A fox trots up the High Street,
explores doorways, clatters dustbins,
takes over the city.

Badger

It is quiet in the woods
Above the town,
And a night breeze stirs
As the sun goes down.

I am looking at a hole
In the side of the hill,
I am hardly even breathing
I am keeping so still.

I can hear the passing traffic
In a sort of distant hum,
I am staring at the hole,
Will the badger ever come?

I can see him – there's his face,
With its clear white stripe,
And his gently rolling body
As he steps into the night.

He pauses just a moment,
Lifts his head to sniff the air,
Then he melts into the trees
Like a shadow, like a prayer.

It is quiet in the woods
And the light has almost gone,
But I have seen a badger,
My very first one.

Robosaurus – King of the Scrap-yard

I'm an eater of metal,
I thrive on the taste,
So bring on your rubbish,
Bring on your waste.

I can scrunch a family car,
I can tear apart a plane,
I can crush a giant liner
Or an express train.

I eat buses for my breakfast,
I eat tractors for a snack,
And once they're in my claws
There is no going back.

Now I'm getting very hungry
And I'm coming near to you,
If you haven't any old stuff
Then I'll have to eat the new –

Hiccup. . .Oops. . .

This new stuff's really horrid,
I didn't enjoy a thing,
I really must remember
I'm the Scrap-yard King!

Cows Moo, Cars Toot

In the street,
   cars toot,
   bicycle-bells ring,
   pelican crossings beep.

By the station,
   trains clatter,
   people chatter,
   children shout.

In the supermarket,
   babies cry,
   tills ting,
   trolleys rumble.

Sounds amazing,
   but what is it like
   in the countryside?